ROBERT F.X. SILLERMAN and **MEL BROOKS**

in association with

THE R/F/B/V GROUP

Present

THE NEW
mel brooks
musical

YOUNG FRANKENSTEIN

Book by **MEL BROOKS** and **THOMAS MEEHAN**   Music and Lyrics by **MEL BROOKS**

Based on the story and screenplay by GENE WILDER and MEL BROOKS and on the original motion picture by special arrangement with TWENTIETH CENTURY FOX

Starring

ROGER BART   **MEGAN MULLALLY**

SUTTON FOSTER   **SHULER HENSLEY**   **ANDREA MARTIN**

FRED APPLEGATE   **CHRISTOPHER FITZGERALD**

With

HEATHER AYERS   **JIM BORSTELMANN**   **PAUL CASTREE**

JACK DOYLE   **KEVIN LIGON**   **LINDA MUGLESTON**

JENNIFER LEE CROWL   **RENÉE FEDER**   **JAMES GRAY**   **AMY HEGGINS**   **ERIC JACKSON**

KRISTIN MARIE JOHNSON   **MATTHEW LABANCA**   **BARRETT MARTIN**   **CHRISTINA MARIE NORRUP**   **JUSTIN PATTERSON**

BRIAN SHEPARD   **SARRAH STRIMEL**   **CRAIG WALETZKO**   **COURTNEY YOUNG**

Scenery Designed by
ROBIN WAGNER

Costumes Designed by
WILLIAM IVEY LONG

Lighting Designed by
PETER KACZOROWSKI

Sound Designed by
JONATHAN DEANS

Special Effects Designed by
MARC BRICKMAN

Wigs & Hair Designed by
PAUL HUNTLEY

Make Up Designed by
ANGELINA AVALLONE

Casting by
TARA RUBIN CASTING

Associate Director
STEVEN ZWEIGBAUM

Associate Choreographer
CHRIS PETERSON

Music Direction and Vocal Arrangements by
PATRICK S. BRADY

Orchestrations by
DOUG BESTERMAN

Music Coordination by
JOHN MILLER

General Management
RICHARD FRANKEL PRODUCTIONS
LAURA GREEN

Technical Supervision
HUDSON THEATRICAL ASSOCIATES

Press Representative
BARLOW · HARTMAN

Associate Producer
ONE VIKING PRODUCTIONS
CARL PASBJERG

Music Arrangements & Supervision by
GLEN KELLY

Direction & Choreography by
SUSAN STROMAN

"Puttin' On The Ritz" by IRVING BERLIN

Proudly Sponsored by Fidelity Investments

Cover art courtesy of SpotCo

ISBN 978-1-4234-3981-3

7777 W. BLUEMOUND RD. P.O. BOX 13819 MILWAUKEE, WI 53213

In Australia Contact:
Hal Leonard Australia Pty. Ltd.
4 Lentara Court
Cheltenham, Victoria, 3192 Australia
Email: ausadmin@halleonard.com.au

Visit Hal Leonard Online at
www.halleonard.com

CONTENTS

THE HAPPIEST TOWN

Music and Lyrics by
MEL BROOKS

Lyrics:

down now. _____ Now the doc - tor's passed. We're

free at last! We're the hap - pi - est town in

town! On this hap - py day we

say, "A - men." We have want - ed this since

THE BRAIN

Music and Lyrics by
MEL BROOKS

deal in fact, not fic-tion. I am a sci-en-tist. I live for truth and rea-son. That's the rea-son I ex-

Faster

ist.

FREDERICK: *There is a vast difference between my crazy grandfather's delusional experiments and my own devotion to pure science. Which leads us directly to the subject of today's lecture.*

The

(vamp)

brain!

There is noth-ing like the brain.

Hearts and lungs are simp-ly tin-ker toys ___ when stacked a - gainst the

PLEASE DON'T TOUCH ME

Music and Lyrics by
MEL BROOKS

please _____ don't touch me. _____

ELIZABETH: *Freddy, I know that you're a virgin…*
FREDERICK: *Yes, a virgin and proud of it!*
For me, science has always come first.
ELIZABETH: *… and as every guy in New York knows,*
I come first, too.

ELIZABETH:
Af - ter our

wed - ding, you'll be, oh, so glad we wait - ed. Un -

til then take cold show - ers when you're o - ver - stim - u -

B♭13 6fr
B13 7fr
C13 2fr
D♭13 3fr
dare to touch our tits, to touch our tits, to touch our tits, to touch our
D♭7 4fr
ELIZABETH:
tits, tits, tits, tits, tits, tits, tits, tits,
G G6 Gmaj7 G6 G G♯dim7
tits!
f
Am7 D7
Our tits!

When we're ab-so-lute-ly wed, you can

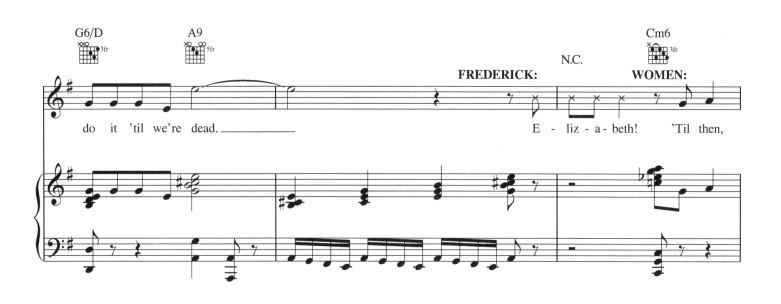

do it 'til we're dead. _____ E - liz - a - beth! 'Til then,

FREDERICK: N.C.   WOMEN:

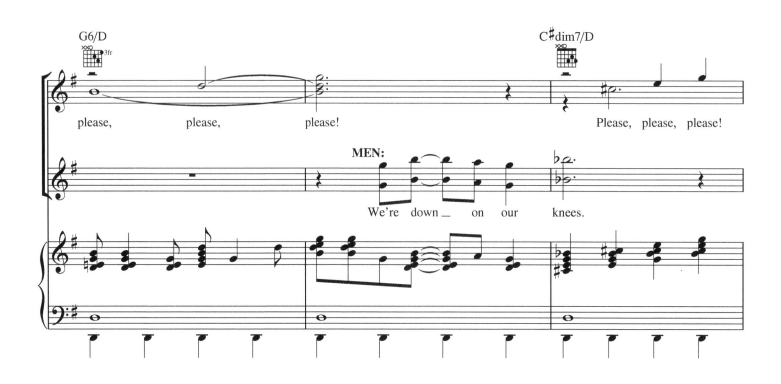

please,   please,   please!   Please, please, please!

MEN:

We're down _ on our knees.

TOGETHER AGAIN

Music and Lyrics by
MEL BROOKS

* Frederick hits Igor's hump

ROLL IN THE HAY

Music and Lyrics by
MEL BROOKS

Rustic Waltz

Bb   Bbmaj7   Bb6   G7   C7

F7   Bb   F7   Bb6

INGA:

Roll,   roll,

Bdim7   Cm7   F7

roll in the hay.   Roll,   roll your

Cm7   F7   Cm7   F7

trou-bles a-way.   When life is aw-ful, just

INGA: *I'm very high-spirited, Doctor. I*
hope you won't hold it against me.
FREDERICK: *Oh! I'll try not to.*

roll in the hay.

Hitch those hors - es up for a gay ride. We'll have

lots of fun. Noth - ing's bet - ter

than a hay - ride un - der - neath the sun.

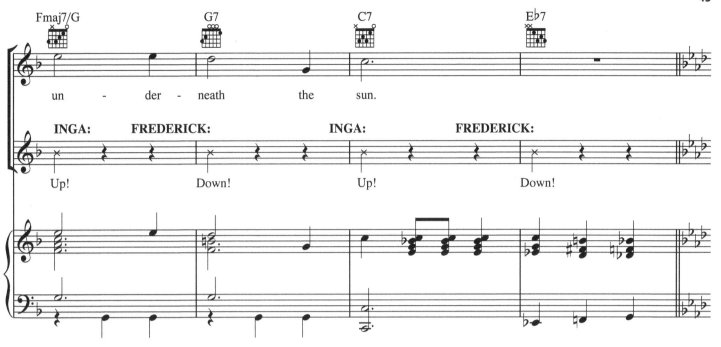

Fmaj7/G   G7   C7   Eb7

un - der - neath the sun.

INGA: FREDERICK: INGA: FREDERICK:

Up!   Down!   Up!   Down!

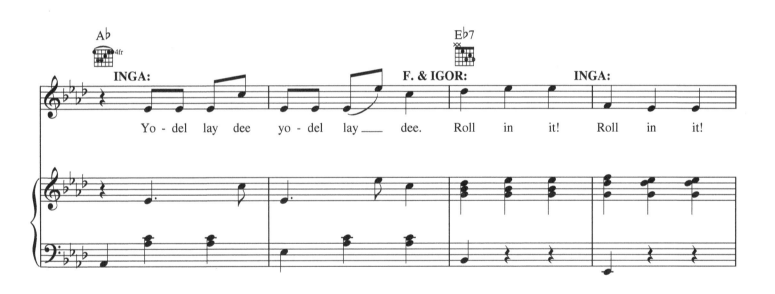

Ab   Eb7

INGA: F. & IGOR: INGA:

Yo - del lay dee yo - del lay ___ dee. Roll in it! Roll in it!

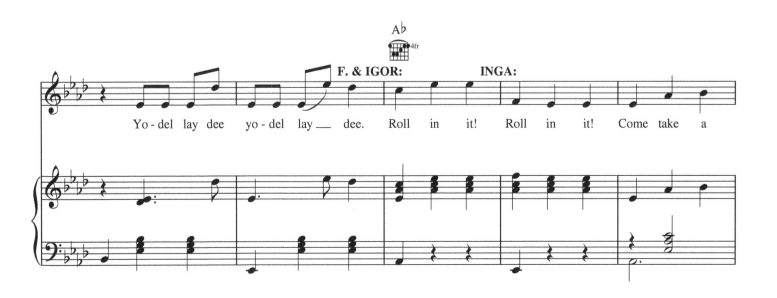

Ab

F. & IGOR: INGA:

Yo - del lay dee yo - del lay ___ dee. Roll in it! Roll in it! Come take a

FREDERICK & IGOR:

Roll - in', __ roll - in', __ roll - in', __ roll - in', __ roll - in', __

ALL:

__ Roll in the hay. __

roll - in'. __

JOIN THE FAMILY BUSINESS

Music and Lyrics by
MEL BROOKS

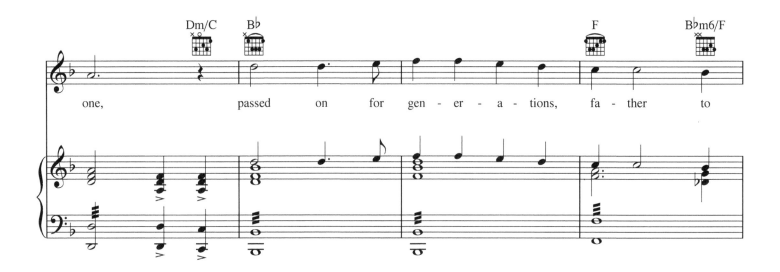

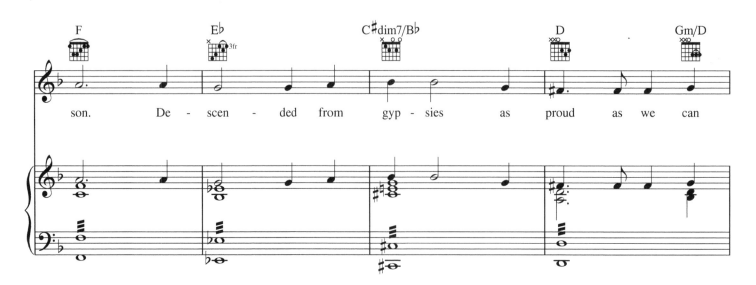

be. Don't risk my curse. It could be worse. Em-brace your fam-'ly tree!

Hungarian Two-Step, moderately fast

Join the fam-'ly bus-'ness, learn a fam-'ly trade, make your-self a mon-ster, make the world a-fraid! Join the fam-'ly bus-'ness, you must

HE VAS MY BOYFRIEND

Music and Lyrics by
MEL BROOKS

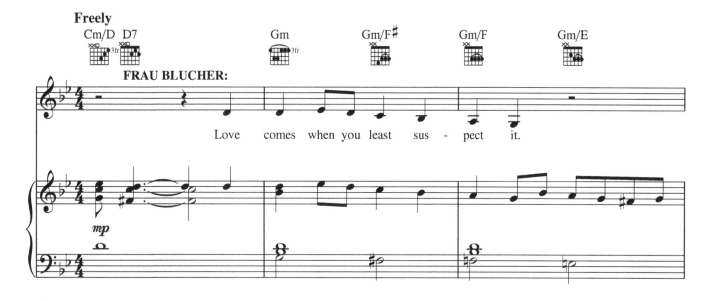

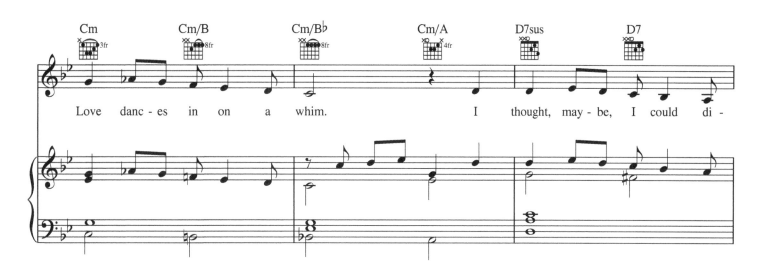

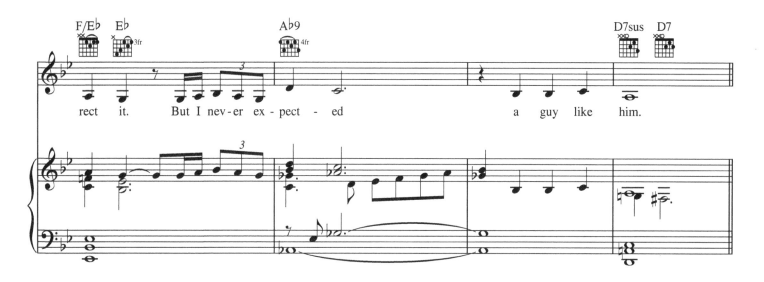

Tempo di Weill

he vas a dirty old goat. Ve vere made for each other. All of a sudden, he took out his paraphernalia and shouted, "Let's play croquet!" And off to the field ve vent. He carried his hoops and mallets and I carried his balls. What a festival! Fun and games all day long. Archery, badminton, potato sack. Victor won the three-legged race… all by himself.

It vas love at first sight.

He vas the one who I

gave my heart to, but ve nev-er wed, e-ven so.

If I men-tioned wed-lock, he'd put me in a head-lock.

LIFE, LIFE

Music and Lyrics by
MEL BROOKS

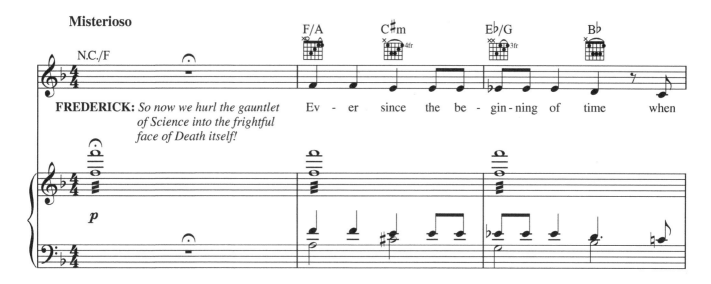

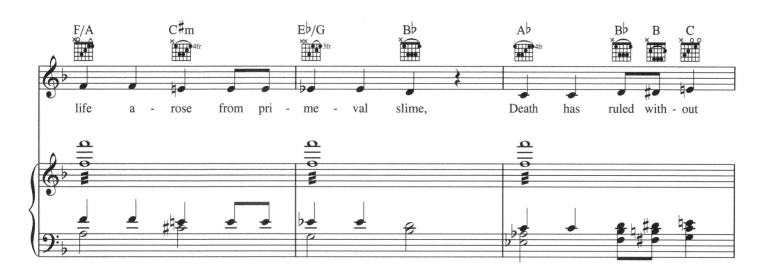

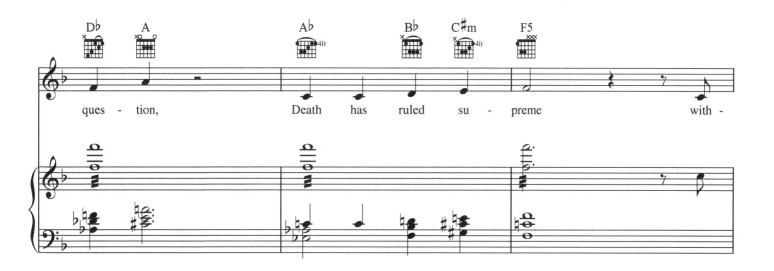

Fate, fate, give my crea-ture life. Give my crea-ture

through the storm and strife. _____ Give the crea-ture life.

rall.

Molto agitato

C#m

D+/E

life.

FREDERICK: *This is it! Igor, throw the first switch!*
IGOR: *Yes, master!*

f *p (vamp)* *ff*

8vb _____

C#7#5

FREDERICK:

Life, life,

f

light-ning bolts and thun-der will ig - nite a mor-tal spark.

FREDERICK: *Now, Igor, throw the third switch!*
IGOR: *Not the third switch!*
FREDERICK: *Yes, the third switch! Throw it, damn you, throw it!*

IGOR: *Yes, master!*

FREDERICK: *Inga, now!*

(vamp)

Slower, with passion

FREDERICK:

Em

N.C.

Give me life _____ ere the break of

INGA, FRAU BLUCHER,
IGOR, WOMEN & TENORS:

Life, life, ere the break of dawn.

BASSES:

Life, life, ere the break of dawn.

rall.

ff

WELCOME TO TRANSYLVANIA

Music and Lyrics by
MEL BROOKS

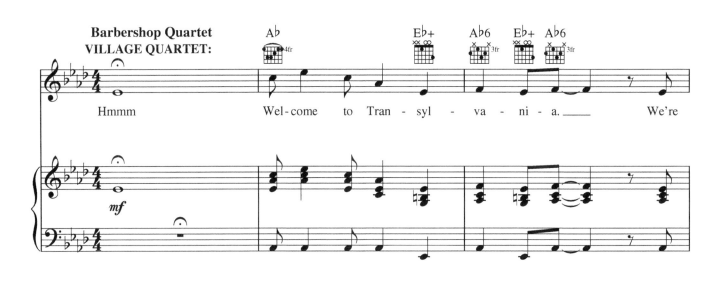

Barbershop Quartet
VILLAGE QUARTET:

Hmmm   Wel-come to Tran - syl - va - ni - a.____   We're

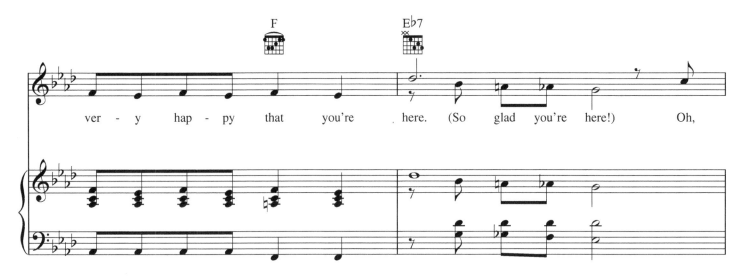

ver - y hap - py that you're here. (So glad you're here!)   Oh,

wel - come to Tran - syl - va - ni - a._____   We

TRANSYLVANIA MANIA

Music and Lyrics by
MEL BROOKS

MONSTER: *Ooooooooo...*
FREDERICK: *The Monster's awake! We've got to come up*
with some sort of diversion, and fast before...
MONSTER: *Ooooooooo...*

Freely

IGOR:

Oh, for - get a - bout the fox -

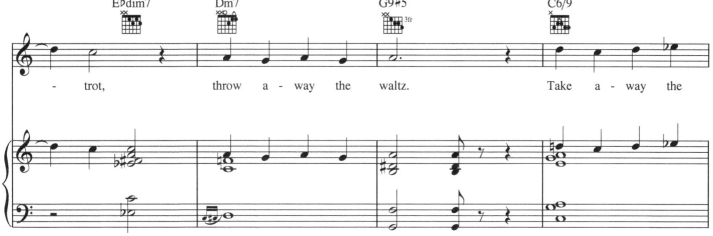

- trot, throw a - way the waltz. Take a - way the

two - step and all that oth - er schmaltz. **MONSTER:** *Ahrrrrrr... Are* you

LISTEN TO YOUR HEART

Music and Lyrics by
MEL BROOKS

1930s Cole Porter Beguine, not too fast

SURPRISE

Music and Lyrics by
MEL BROOKS

PLEASE SEND ME SOMEONE

Music and Lyrics by
MEL BROOKS

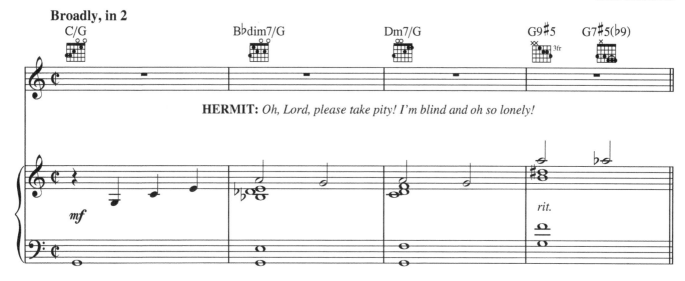

HERMIT: *Oh, Lord, please take pity! I'm blind and oh so lonely!*

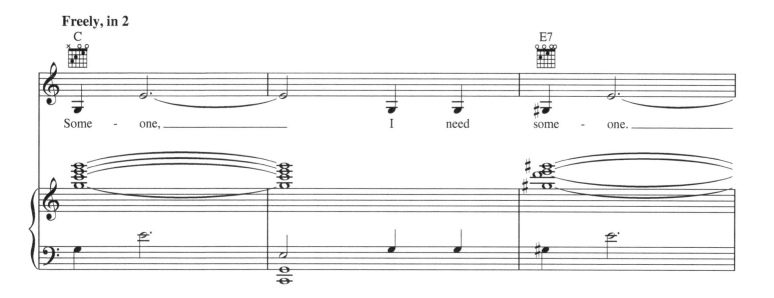

Some - one,_____ I need some - one._____

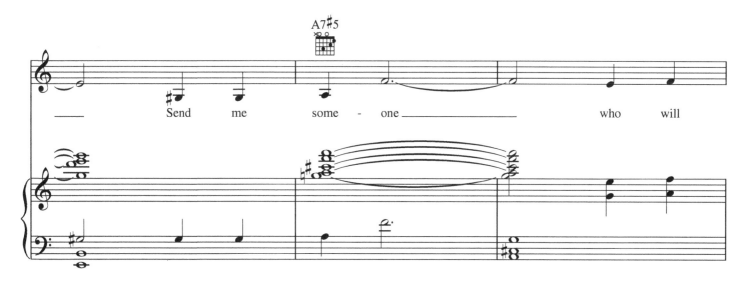

_____ Send me some - one _____ who will

MAN ABOUT TOWN

Music and Lyrics by
MEL BROOKS

Andante

FREDERICK: Now, you're a crea-ture, a prim-i-tive soul. You don't know your left from your right. ___ You're

lost in the dark. You need a spark to lead you in-to the light.

I'll be that guide, I'll be by your side. I'll pull you out of the mire.

112

PUTTIN' ON THE RITZ

Words and Music by
IRVING BERLIN

INGA & IGOR:

Ritz, put - tin' on the Ritz!

DEEP LOVE

Music and Lyrics by
MEL BROOKS

Freely

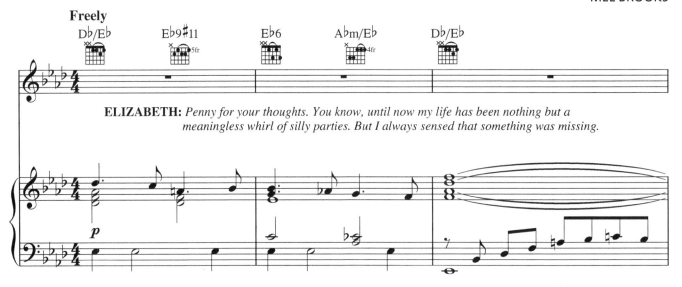

ELIZABETH: *Penny for your thoughts. You know, until now my life has been nothing but a meaningless whirl of silly parties. But I always sensed that something was missing.*

Love!   And I'm not talking about puppy love, either, one-night stand love or cheap love.   No!

Andante

What I'm talkin' about is… what's the word I'm looking for?… Oh, yes…

ALONE

Music and Lyrics by
MEL BROOKS

Bright 4

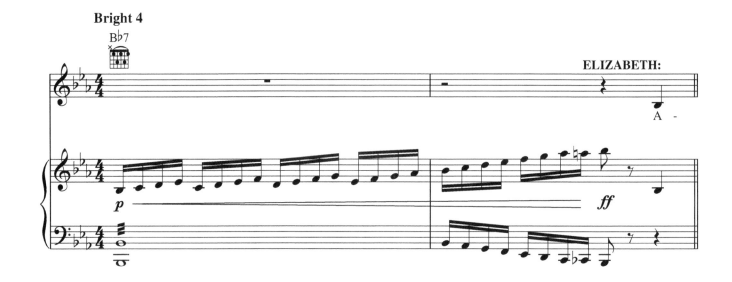

ELIZABETH:

A -

Cole Porter-ish Bequine

lone _____ on my French iv-'ry phone,

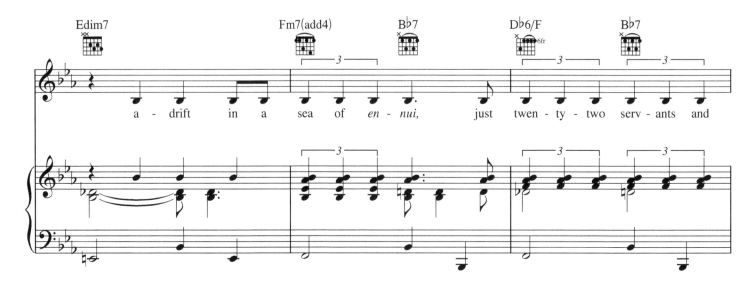

a - drift in a sea of *en - nui,* just twen-ty-two serv-ants and

WELCOME TO TRANSYLVANIA

Music and Lyrics by
MEL BROOKS